MW00654125

Be **STILL** AND *Know*
THAT I AM GOD

Be STILL AND Know THAT I AM GOD

DAILY DEVOTIONS AND EMERGENCY PRAYERS

GINA WASHINGTON

TATE PUBLISHING
AND ENTERPRISES, LLC

Published by Tate Publishing & Enterprises, LLC
127 E. Trade Center Terrace | Mustang, Oklahoma 73064 USA
1.888.361.9473 | www.tatepublishing.com

Tate Publishing is committed to excellence in the publishing industry. The company reflects the philosophy established by the founders, based on Psalm 68:11,
"The Lord gave the word and great was the company of those who published it."

Book design copyright © 2013 by Tate Publishing, LLC. All rights reserved.
Cover design by Junriel Boquecosa
Interior design by Jake Muelle

Published in the United States of America

ISBN: 978-1-62854-227-1
1. Religion / Christian Life / Devotional
2. Religion / Christian Life / Prayer
13.11.01

DEDICATION

*T*his book is dedicated to my amazing, smart, faithful, and prayerful daughter, Vivian Faith Washington. Thank you for your support and motivation to encourage others. Your encouragement has been a blessing. I am grateful that God has entrusted me to raise such an amazing and resilient daughter.

TABLE OF CONTENTS

INTRODUCTION

*H*ave you ever felt alone while in the midst of a crisis? Had you ever felt like no one understood the hurt you were feeling? Have you felt the need to pray but didn't know how to pray because the pain was so severe? Have you felt the need for encouragement but didn't know where to go? Perhaps you have gone through a divorce, lost a loved one, or lost a job. This devotional for painful situations will assist you in your walk to become stronger and encouraged. The prayers will offer you somewhere to go in the midst of turmoil and challenge you to become stronger after facing a crisis scenario. A crisis could mean losing a job, a loved one dying, going through a divorce, dealing with addiction, hurt from a past relationship, stress from single parenting, etc. This devotional will offer you a prayer to identify your pain, steps to move past the pain, prayer to seek God's help, and a scripture to encourage you. After reading each devotional, my prayer is that you feel closer to God, you feel a sense of peace and calmness, and you are ready to do the work for your healing. I encourage you to journal along while reading and use the blank pages at the end of each devotion to write down your thoughts and action steps needed to move from hurt to healing.

SECTION 1: FAITH

"Lord, I need more faith! Everything around me seems to crumble and nothing seems to be going right! Dear Lord I need your help right now!"

*I*t may be hard to see right at this moment but you must believe that God is right by your side. Call on God and tell Him you need more faith. Tell Him everything and confess that you need more faith. Jesus is the way, the truth, and the light. Once you get alone with Him and let your stresses and fears out, you can defeat what you are also willing to confront.

"Dear Lord, I am in need of more faith. I thank you in advance for enlarging my territory and giving me more faith. You said we just needed faith that is as small as a mustard seed, so I declare that in your name I have more faith. Amen."

> Faith is the confidence that what we hope for will actually happen; it gives us assurance about things we cannot see.
>
> Hebrews 11:1 (NLT)

Gina Washington

JOURNAL APPLICATION:

Take a moment and get alone with God: take a walk, get
somewhere quiet, and take slow breaths of air. Write down
a prayer to receive more faith.

_____

_____

_____

_____

_____

_____

_____

_____

_____

_____

_____

_____

_____

_____

_____

SECTION 1: FAITH

"I have been emotionally abused; I have been called nothing and made to feel like nothing by someone whom I love. My self-image has been destroyed. My confidence level is minimal. Now what?"

God loves you and knows the way you take! God knows all about your life and He has never left your side. God's desire for you is to walk in self-confidence and joy. Hold your head up high and declare that God will restore your self-image. He will restore and heal all of the scars that you have. Hold on and trust that God holds the key to your restoration!

"Dear Lord, please take this negative self-image away. Keep me focused on your promises. I believe that my confidence level will soar. I trust that no one can judge me except you, and that my spirit will show I am fearfully and wonderfully made. Amen."

> Thank you for making me so wonderfully complex! Your workmanship is marvelous—how well I know it.
>
> Psalm 139:14 (NLT)

Gina Washington

JOURNAL APPLICATION:

Write down three things that are unique about you. Each day for a year, add a new characteristic that makes you unique. At the end of the year, review your "uniqueness characteristics." Anytime you need encouragement review your uniqueness journal entries.

_____

_____

_____

_____

_____

_____

_____

_____

_____

_____

_____

_____

_____

_____

_____

_____

SECTION 1: FAITH

"Lord, I am in need to go higher in my worship experience. The church I am at is not fulfilling that need. I have been here for several years. Help!"

*P*ray before leaving your church. Ask God for guidance and direction. God wants to give you the desires of your heart. If you aren't being spiritually fed evaluate the situation and after prayer and spiritual guidance, go where the Holy Spirit leads you. Being in a worship setting that is preaching the good news is essential for spiritual growth. However, that spiritual growth starts with you. You can't expect someone else to usher your worship experience to you. Worship starts in the heart.

"Dear Lord, fill my heart with a worship experience. Give me an attitude of gratitude and order my steps. I don't want to be out of your will. Show me your will and fill me with a worship attitude. Feed my spirit with the good news and teach me to receive it. Amen."

> If you need wisdom, ask our generous God, and he will give it to you. He will not rebuke you for asking.
>
> James 1:5 (NLT)

Gina Washington

JOURNAL APPLICATION:

Write down five ways to become a better worshipper.

_____
_____
_____
_____
_____
_____
_____
_____
_____
_____
_____
_____
_____
_____
_____
_____
_____
_____

SECTION 1: FAITH

"Lord I am so tired, I have worked a full day and all I want to do is relax. However, there are people that depend on me and need me. I need more physical, emotional, and spiritual energy to get everything done. I am overwhelmed. Help!"

"Dear Lord, thank you in advance for increasing my energy level. I need energy that is more than enough. I need energy that will allow me to be a blessing to someone else. Lord, I thank you in advance for this new energy! Amen."

> But those who trust in the Lord will find new strength. They will soar high on wings like eagles. They will run and not grow weary. They will walk and not faint.

Isaiah 40:31 (NLT)

JOURNAL APPLICATION:

Write down three ways in each area that you can receive
more energy. Ex: I can walk more to increase my physical
energy, I can attend bible study on a regular basis to receive
more spiritual energy, and I can stop worrying so much to
increase my emotional stability.

_____

_____

_____

_____

_____

_____

_____

_____

_____

_____

_____

_____

_____

_____

SECTION 1: FAITH

"I need spiritual energy! I know unless you reside in my soul, I can't keep pouring out and pouring out without your energy."

*G*et up and start worshipping God. Find a song you like and sing it to God. Sometimes all you need is a "Thank you Jesus" to start moving and praising. It's not about what you're doing wrong but more about what you're willing to do right. Start your day off with God in prayer and you are sure to get results. You get spiritual energy by spending time with God.

"Dear Lord, thank you in advance for increasing my will to want to spend more time with you. The more time I spend with you, the more time I want to be alone with you. I receive this new Spiritual energy. In your name I pray. Amen."

> Shout with joy to the Lord, all the earth! Worship the Lord with gladness. Come before him, singing with joy. Acknowledge that the Lord is God. He made us, and we are his. We are his people, the sheep of his pasture. Enter his gates with thanksgiving; go into his courts with praise. Give thanks to him and praise his name. For the Lord is good. His unfailing love continues forever, and his faithfulness continues to each generation.
>
> Psalms 100:1-5 (NLT)

JOURNAL APPLICATION:

Write down the words from your favorite praise/worship song and sing the song whenever you are in need of more spiritual energy.

_____

_____

_____

_____

_____

_____

_____

_____

_____

_____

_____

_____

_____

_____

_____

_____

SECTION 1: FAITH

"Lord, I need to establish a healthy lifestyle. I am not eating food that is nourishment for my body. I must confess, I am eating what tastes good not what feels good. I need a change. I am ready for a change and need your help!"

Commit to eating healthier and to include more fruits and vegetables in your diet. Seek ye first the kingdom of God and His righteousness. God wants the best for you and He knows what is best for you. You must support yourself with becoming healthier: exercise (walk) more, choose healthier foods, and pray for guidance through this process. When you are healthier, the people around you become healthier.

"Dear Lord, I know that becoming healthy is a choice. I am deciding today that I want a healthier life: physically, emotionally, and spiritually. I confess that my body and mind have not been committed to healthiness. However, today I choose life! And that means healthiness for my mind, body, spirit, and soul. Amen."

> So whether you eat or drink, or whatever you do, do it all for the glory of God.
>
> 1 Corinthians 10:31 (NLT)

Gina Washington

JOURNAL APPLICATION:

Write down the ways in which you plan to become healthier.
Call this your "healthy action plan." Ex: I plan to read my
bible daily, walk at least fifteen minutes daily, and I plan to
eat a fruit and/or a vegetable daily.

_____

_____

_____

_____

_____

_____

_____

_____

_____

_____

_____

_____

_____

SECTION 1: FAITH

"Lord, I have been blessed so swiftly and abundantly. Reality has hit me that you will open up the windows of heaven and pour out a blessing that I will not have room enough to receive. I am walking in guilt because I have abundance. Please forgive me, but although I had faith as small as a mustard seed, this blessing blew my mind. How can I get rid of this guilt? Dear Lord, please take the guilt away from me. Help."

*G*od promises you a blessing that will overflow. Don't feel guilty for the favor of God in your life. The Holy Spirit has paid you a visit and is working on your behalf. Take yourself out of your blessing and give God all the honor and praise. When the praises go up the blessings have to come down.

"Dear God, thank you, thank you, thank you for blessing me! Create a thankful spirit within me, so that others see the glory and blessings you have given to me. Amen."

> For God has not given us a spirit of fear and timidity, but of power, love, and self-discipline.
>
> 2 Timothy 1:7 (NLT)

> Bring all the tithes into the storehouse so there will be enough food in my Temple. If you do," says the

Lord of Heaven's Armies, "I will open the windows of heaven for you. I will pour out a blessing so great you won't have enough room to take it in! Try it! Put me to the test!

Malachi 3:10 (NLT)

JOURNAL APPLICATION:

Write down daily ten things you are grateful for.

_____

_____

_____

_____

_____

_____

_____

_____

_____

_____

_____

_____

_____

_____

_____

_____

_____

_____

SECTION 1: FAITH

"Lord, today I pray for myself. I often lend myself to others for support. It's my turn to pray for myself. I simply pray for increase and that you would enlarge my territory. Amen."

God is a rewarder of those that diligently seek Him. Keep the faith, be encouraged, and keep seeking Him.

Dear God, I pray for favor, peace, and unspeakable joy over my life. Take away the guilt I feel when I pray for myself. Amen."

> He was the one who prayed to the God of Israel, "Oh, that you would bless me and expand my territory! Please be with me in all that I do, and keep me from all trouble and pain!" And God granted him his request.
>
> 1 Chronicles 4:10 (NLT)

JOURNAL APPLICATION:

Write a letter to yourself explaining how much you love yourself. Write a "prayer of promise" to do three things for yourself weekly.

_____

_____

_____

_____

_____

_____

_____

_____

_____

_____

_____

_____

_____

_____

_____

_____

SECTION 1: FAITH

"I need to be loved. I realize that first I must love others the way God loves me. Dear Lord, help me to have love for others in my heart at all times. I pray that you increase my heart to love others who are different from me. Increase my tolerance for diversity in all aspects of my life. Amen."

God allows diversity in our life to show His unconditional love for everyone. Love is an action word, it requires that you do something. Love is patient, kind, long-suffering, it does not keep a record of wrongs. To love someone completely means you accept them wholeheartedly. Love means accepting the differences of others. Love conquers all.

"Dear God, I desire to love others the way you have shown me love. Allow me to walk in love daily, without second guessing myself. I love you God more than anything and my greatest desire is to please you by loving others. Amen."

> Love is patient and kind. Love is not jealous or boastful or proud or rude. It does not demand its own way. It is not irritable, and it keeps no record of being wronged. It does not rejoice about injustice but rejoices whenever the truth wins out. Love never gives up, never loses faith, is always hopeful, and endures through every circumstance.
>
> 1 Corinthians 13:4-7 (NLT)

JOURNAL APPLICATION:

Write down ten ways you can express love.

_____
_____
_____
_____
_____
_____
_____
_____
_____
_____
_____
_____
_____
_____
_____
_____
_____
_____
_____

SECTION 2: LONELINESS

"Lord, I am impatient and frustrated that you have not sent me a mate yet! All of my friends have spouses and I have attended more weddings than I can count, when will it be my turn? Will you ever send me a spouse?"

*J*ust because you have attended more weddings than you can count doesn't mean God has forgotten you. Everything in life worth having is a process. In the bible, Ruth worked in the fields picking grains and concentrated on providing for her family (ex-mother-in-law). While she was working and minding her own business, Boaz was watching her. Eventually, this rich owner of the fields ended up marrying Ruth. God had ordained this union before they were married. Ruth respected the process of working and taking care of her former mother-in-law while waiting. She respected the process. Respect the process that God is taking you through.

"Dear Lord, calm my nerves while I am waiting. Please give me more patience and peace while I wait. Amen."

> Wait patiently for the Lord. Be brave and courageous. Yes, wait patiently for the Lord.
>
> Psalm 27:14 (NLT)

JOURNAL APPLICATION:

Write down ten things that you want in a spouse. Ask yourself, are you willing to give those ten things? How can you respect the process while waiting for a spouse? Ex: join a Christian singles ministry.

_____

_____

_____

_____

_____

_____

_____

_____

_____

_____

_____

_____

_____

_____

SECTION 2: LONELINESS

"Lord I need a breakthrough! I am tired of feeling lonely! I am around many people yet I still have a sense of loneliness. I want someone to love me just for me and respect the love that I give them in return. I need patience. Help!"

The Lord will supply all of your needs according to His riches in glory. Hold on and be grateful for the people He sends your way. Create a prayer list of positive people in your life and ask God to allow your heart and mind to accept them.

"Dear Lord, take away the impatient feelings that I am having. Create in me a spirit of joy, hope, and faith. Help me not to have feelings of loneliness while I am with others. Allow me, dear God, to be in the present and to feel the presence and love of others. I will gratefully receive the family and friends that you have designed just for me. I am thankful. Amen.

> Rejoice in our confident hope. Be patient in trouble, and keep on praying.
>
> Romans 12:12 (NLT)

Gina Washington

JOURNAL APPLICATION:

Write down an agreement with yourself that anytime
you are feeling lonely, you will do an activity to alleviate
the feeling. Ex: call a friend who can be accountable to
remind you that you are not lonely, watch a movie, or take
a nature walk.

SECTION 2: LONELINESS

"I am tired of being lonely and going to bed by myself. What's the deal, I thought you were sending me a mate?"

Stop being impatient! God is sending you a spouse not a bed partner. Aren't you tired of unfulfilled relationships with different people walking in and out of your life? You have been praying for the right mate and God hears your prayers. He is molding just the right mate for you that is equally yoked. Be still and know that God is in control!

"Dear Lord, thank you for allowing me to hear your voice. Thank you in advance for preparing and molding my future spouse. I thank you for giving me patience while I wait. I want the right mate and I don't want to have to settle. I want what you want for me. Teach me kindness and resiliency while I wait. Amen."

> I waited patiently for the Lord to help me, and he turned to me and heard my cry.
>
> Psalms 40:1 (NLT)

JOURNAL APPLICATION:

Write down ten ways to be patient while you wait for the right spouse. Review these entries daily and date them so that you are held accountable while you wait.

_____

_____

_____

_____

_____

_____

_____

_____

_____

_____

_____

_____

_____

_____

_____

_____

SECTION 2: LONELINESS

"Dear God, my spouse has been deployed. Help! I didn't sign up for this. I am in a new environment without my spouse and without my family. I am emotionally drained from the thought of my spouse being in danger. Help!"

Take a deep breath. Take another deep breath. Getting overly excited will only make matters worse. Although you feel you didn't sign up for this, keep in mind your spouse needs you to be strong so that their mind is clear and not worried about you. The time away from your spouse will not be easy, however stay focused and keep your faith. God will never put more on you than you can bear.

"God, I need you now! I need more faith, more patience, more strength, and more peace while away from my spouse. Give me the wisdom to handle the household while away from my spouse. Increase my faith so that when I talk to my spouse I can speak faith into them. Send me friends in this new place and give me new memories to share. Help me to understand that this is only for a season and not a lifetime. Amen."

> Faith is the confidence that what we hope for will actually happen; it gives us assurance about things we cannot see.
>
> Hebrews 11:1 (NLT)

Gina Washington

JOURNAL APPLICATION:

Write down ten faith statements that you hope will occur during your spouses' time of deployment. Ex. I have faith that our family will enjoy a peaceful and joyous Thanksgiving.

_____

_____

_____

_____

_____

_____

_____

_____

_____

_____

_____

_____

_____

_____

_____

SECTION 3: TRUST

"I have been mistreated and I have trusted someone who treated me horribly and broke that trust. It is now hard for me to trust anyone! Help me because this mistrust is affecting my current relationships."

*A*lthough it may seem difficult to do, take one day at a time and trust God. Tell Him all about the mistrust you are having. Pray specifically that the mistrust can be lifted off of you and God will open your heart to trust again. This may be a slow process but trust that God knows the way that you take.

"Dear Lord, please take this spirit of mistrust out of my life. When I trust you I know that all things are possible for those that believe. Lord, my trust in you will equal my trust in others. Thank you in advance for the spirit of trust that you will bestow upon me. Amen."

> Trust in the Lord with all your heart; do not depend on your own understanding.
>
> Proverbs 3:5 (NLT)

JOURNAL APPLICATION:

Write down the name of the person whom you feel violated
your trust the most. Write them a forgiveness letter. Now
write down a prayer asking God to restore your trust.

_____

_____

SECTION 3: TRUST

"I have not been obedient to the calling in my life. I know that I have a spiritual gift God has given me but it's difficult to use my spiritual gift and still take my place in my family, society, and church. Dear Lord, help me to discover and use my spiritual gifts. Amen."

God has given each of us a gift. Do not be afraid to walk in your gift. God has not given us a spirit of fear. I promise you that God will give you the right circumstances, the right resources, and the right people to operate your gift effectively.

"Dear Lord, show me how to operate in the gift you have given. Allow me to glorify you while operating in my gift. Give me wisdom, faith, and knowledge in my gift. Amen."

> There are different kinds of spiritual gifts, but the same Spirit is the source of them all. There are different kinds of service, but we serve the same Lord. God works in different ways, but it is the same God who does the work in all of us.
>
> 1 Corinthians 12:4-6 (NLT)

JOURNAL APPLICATION:

Write down a prayer for God to reveal the gifts He has for
you. Take a spiritual gifts survey.

_____

_____

_____

_____

_____

_____

_____

_____

_____

_____

_____

_____

_____

_____

_____

_____

_____

_____

SECTION 3: TRUST

"I am dreading a decision that I know I must make! God, I need guidance. I need to stop asking everyone else for help and look to you for my answer. I have tried it my way; I promise you I am now ready to allow you to guide me. Dear Lord, I surrender this entire situation to you. I know that you are able to do exceedingly and abundantly above all that I could ask. Help me to trust you no matter how this turns out. Amen."

Second guessing yourself will only prolong the situation. Asking for guidance and getting quiet so that you can think effectively is imperative.

"Dear God, I know that you are right here. Thank you for guarding my mind and giving me clear direction to make wise decisions. Amen."

> Now all glory to God, who is able, through his mighty power at work within us, to accomplish infinitely more than we might ask or think.
>
> Ephesians 3: 20 (NLT)

JOURNAL APPLICATION:

Write down the decision you are dreading and read it aloud to yourself. Next, write down your prayer for guidance and wisdom. Be sure to write a prayer of thanks when God gives you clarity to make the decision you have been dreading.

_____

_____

_____

_____

_____

_____

_____

_____

_____

_____

_____

_____

_____

_____

_____

SECTION 3: TRUST

"It is time to say goodbye to someone who no longer belongs in my life. I have known for some time that this relationship is toxic and no longer brings me joy. In fact, when I am around this person, I feel sad, in despair, and negative. I know I need to end it. Dear Lord, what is the next step to end this toxic relationship?"

The next step is to pray and seek God for realization that for everything there is a season. The significance of a season means that you must recognize what season of life you are in. Have you been through a season of divorce and now it is your season to find out who you are as a single person? Knowing what season you are walking in will help you recognize who deserves to be in your presence during your season. When you can recognize toxic people, let them go. When you recognize a toxic relationship let it go. Toxic things can hurt you in more ways than one. End it.

"Dear God, show me how to let go of toxic people. I do not want to waste any more time trying to fit someone in my life that doesn't deserve to be there."

> For everything there is a season, a time for every activity under heaven.
>
> Ecclesiastes 3:1 (NLT)

JOURNAL APPLICATION:

Write down the names of any toxic people in your life. Next, write a prayer asking God to heal them.

_____

_____

_____

_____

_____

_____

_____

_____

_____

_____

_____

_____

_____

_____

_____

_____

_____

_____

SECTION 3: TRUST

"I desire peace. I have been unsettled about many things lately and I understand I need peace."

*G*od honors your request. However, He can't honor what is not requested. Make your requests known to God.

"Dear Lord, I declare peace over everything in my life. Please usher in a spirit of peace and let it saturate in my life. Amen."

> Don't worry about anything; instead, pray about everything. Tell God what you need, and thank him for all he has done.
>
> Philippians 4:6 (NLT)

JOURNAL APPLICATION:

Describe three activities that bring you peace. Ex: I take a "peace walk" when I need more peace. I say "peace prayers" when I need more peace.

_____

_____

_____

_____

_____

_____

_____

_____

_____

_____

_____

_____

_____

_____

_____

_____

SECTION 3: TRUST

"I need to confront someone who has hurt me. This person is a family member, I don't want to be a rebel but enough is enough. No one has stepped up to confront this person so they keep being hurtful to everyone in the family. Dear Lord, help me to confront in love. Amen."

Confronting someone in the spirit of transparency and love is effective. Family members are obligated to not just tolerate one another but to love one another. God represents spirit and truth. Walk in spirit and truth, and confront this family member in love.

"Dear God, give me the words to say when I talk to this family member. Create in me a clean heart and a peaceful spirit so that I can walk in love. I pray for this family member that you would soften their heart to receive what I need to say. I pray this makes our family stronger. Amen."

> A servant of the Lord must not quarrel but must be kind to everyone, be able to teach, and be patient with difficult people. Gently instruct those who oppose the truth. Perhaps God will change those people's hearts, and they will learn the truth.
>
> 2 Timothy 2:24-25 (NLT)

JOURNAL APPLICATION:

Write a prayer of strength to confront this family member.

SECTION 4: SICKNESS-CANCER

"This chemo sucks! Seriously, my body feels like it is going to explode with nausea and hot flashes. My taste buds are not working and my hair is falling out! What gives? I can't take much more of this cancer stuff! Help!"

God will never put more on you then than you can bear. Weeping may endure for a night, but joy comes in the morning. Hold on to God's unchanging hand. God is a healer and although we may not like the process, God is faithful.

"Dear Lord, I am grateful that I am alive. I will stop complaining with 'Why me, why me?' and trust you completely to heal my body. Lord, give my mind, spirit, and body the strength to endure chemo. I know later on down the road I will be grateful to chemo, but right now I just need strength to endure and to get to the next phase. In Jesus name I pray, Amen."

> But he was pierced for our rebellion, crushed for our sins. He was beaten so we could be whole. He was whipped so we could be healed.
>
> Isaiah 53:5 (NLT)

Gina Washington

JOURNAL APPLICATION:

Write down ten healing prayers. When the pain hits, say those "breath prayers." Ex: "Lord give me comfort to endure," "Lord take the flashes away so that I can get to sleep," "Lord if I get sick and throw up, give me strength to keep the next meal down." When I was a caregiver for my baby sister who had breast cancer and endured chemo; our family wrote down healing prayers for her to read during difficult times with chemo.

_____
_____
_____
_____
_____
_____
_____
_____
_____
_____
_____
_____

SECTION 4: SICKNESS

"The spirit of addiction has affected someone in my family. It is difficult to watch this person self-sabotage themselves. If something doesn't quickly turn around this person will not make it. Everyone in the family is affected by this person's actions. I know addiction is a serious stronghold. Please help."

*N*ever lose the faith. The person with the addiction is struggling. Seeking professional assistance with addiction is very important. Even if the person with the addiction is refusing, family members should still seek assistance for themselves. You will have to make a difficult decision on whether or not this person can be in your life throughout this battle. Make that decision through prayer. The good news is that you are now ready to confront this issue. (Resources for families dealing with addiction are located in the appendix.)

"Dear God, I surrender my loved one to you. I pray that you break every chain of addiction that resonates in their body. Heal our family from hurts from this loved one and let this healing process occur in your perfect will. In your name I pray. Amen."

> The temptations in your life are no different from what others experience. And God is faithful. He

will not allow the temptation to be more than you can stand. When you are tempted, he will show you a way out so that you can endure.

1 Corinthians 10:13 (NLT)

JOURNAL APPLICATION:

Write your loved one a "prayer letter." This letter should include your prayer to see them healed from addiction and you should confess your love for them.

_____

_____

_____

_____

_____

_____

_____

_____

_____

_____

_____

_____

_____

_____

_____

_____

_____

SECTION 4: SICKNESS

"Lord, I am struggling with an addiction and I want this stronghold of Satan out of my life. Dear Lord, help!"

God receives your petition and recognizes the stronghold. Each day will require steps toward a life without addiction. Recognize that there may be setbacks but keep the faith and keep your hand in God's unchanging hand. Please reach out for professional assistance (there are resources located in the appendix).

"Dear God, I acknowledge you and the resources you have provided for me to overcome this addiction. Please guide me, direct me, and cultivate me through this process. Keep my family together and as you heal me, please heal my family from the hurt that my addiction has caused. Amen."

> For we are not fighting against flesh-and-blood enemies, but against evil rulers and authorities of the unseen world, against mighty powers in this dark world, and against evil spirits in the heavenly places.
>
> Ephesians 6:12 (NLT)

JOURNAL APPLICATION:

Write down addictions that you are dealing with. Next, write a prayer confronting these addictions and proclaiming a healing.

_____

_____

_____

_____

_____

_____

_____

_____

_____

_____

_____

_____

_____

_____

_____

_____

SECTION 4: SICKNESS

"God, I am a caregiver for a loved one and I am overwhelmed with their sickness. I want to be as supportive as possible yet my faith is dwindling. Please hear my prayer and do not allow my loved one to see my doubts. They depend on me for encouragement and care. Amen."

Caring for a sick loved one can be difficult. If you need help, do not be afraid to say so. Your emotional and physical well-being is important. Keep the faith and take one day at a time. It is important that your life be equally balanced. Do not feel guilty for having other things to do outside of caring for your loved one. It is healthy.

"Dear God, guide my footsteps and order my steps in this situation. I need strength that only you can give. I need patience and wisdom to make smart choices. I need strength to care for my loved one in their time of need. Thank you in advance for increase in strength. Amen."

> Trust in the Lord with all your heart; do not depend on your own understanding.

> Proverbs 3:5

JOURNAL APPLICATION:

Write down ten things that you enjoy. Make a promise to
yourself to do at least three activities from your list weekly.

_____

_____

_____

_____

_____

_____

_____

_____

_____

_____

_____

_____

_____

_____

_____

_____

_____

_____

SECTION 5: DIVORCE

"I am broke! This divorce has devastated me financially. Help!"

Face reality, you may have to start over financially. Your lifestyle may have to change. God will never leave you nor forsake you. God will meet all of your financial needs. You must trust that God is a rewarder of those who diligently seek Him!

"Dear Lord, please cover my finances. I pray for guidance, wisdom, and direction in this area of my life. I am starting over financially and need your guidance. Please send the right resources to me at the right time. Amen."

> And it is impossible to please God without faith. Anyone who wants to come to him must believe that God exists and that he rewards those who sincerely seek him.
>
> Hebrews 11:6 (NLT)

> And this same God who takes care of me will supply all your needs from his glorious riches, which have been given to us in Christ Jesus.
>
> Philippians 4:19 (NLT)

Gina Washington

JOURNAL APPLICATION:

Prepare a budget. At the top of the budget write down
Mark 9:23 (All things are possible for them that believe).
Now identify areas that are non-negotiables (ex: food,
shelter, transportation). Now other items that are negotiable
re-work or delete them from the budget until more income
comes in.

_____
_____
_____
_____
_____
_____
_____
_____
_____
_____
_____
_____
_____
_____

SECTION 5: MARRIAGE

"I want out of this dead marriage. God, I have been miserable for years. Dear Lord, please help! Amen."

God will answer your prayers. Never stay in an unsafe situation. Seek out God for guidance and direction. Let Him order and direct your path! God does not desire for you to be in an unhappy marriage. However, seeking counseling and restoration for your marriage is essential. Many marriages hit rough patches throughout the years. God is a restorer of even the most horrific situations. Being equally yoked is the first step to a successful marriage. Reviewing your marriage and agreeing to communicate positively will lead you to the next steps. Never give up without a fight. However, do not compromise your walk as a Christian while trying to restore your relationship. Seek help for your marriage.

"Dear Lord, please help this broken marriage. I feel like there is no hope and I am becoming bitter. Others are starting to notice my behavior changing. Help me. Change my attitude and heart to see what you see, Lord. Give me signs to hang in there. Send me resources and help for my spouse and I to stay focused on our marriage. Teach me and my spouse to see what you see for our marriage. Touch our family who is being affected by our marriage. I trust you to show me the path to take. Amen."

> Seek the Kingdom of God above all else, and live righteously, and he will give you everything you need.
>
> Matthew 6:33

JOURNAL APPLICATION:

Write down as many positive things about your spouse that you can think of. Go back to when you first got married if need be. Now pray that God will restore and add some more positive attributes to your marriage. Write a prayer of restoration for your marriage.

_____

_____

_____

_____

_____

_____

_____

_____

_____

_____

_____

_____

_____

_____

SECTION 6: FINANCES AND LOSS OF JOB

"Lord, I have been fired from my job. Now what? How dare they cut my position without notifying me earlier."

Take a deep breath and release. Then take another deep breath! Now hold your head up and act gracefully, because the last thing you want to do is seek revenge. Instead, leave peacefully; you may need a recommendation later on. Once you stop your emotions from overwhelming you, get back in the game and move. God never closes a door without opening another one.

"Dear Lord, you know my heart and the dedication that I have given to this job. You know that there were many times I desired to be with my family, yet I was working overtime and not being compensated fairly. Please take the bitterness out of my heart, please take the desire for revenge out of my spirit, and please give me grace to leave this chapter of my life peacefully. You have always supplied my needs according to your riches and glory. I need more faith than ever right now. In your name I pray, Amen."

> "Be still, and know that I am God! I will be honored by every nation. I will be honored throughout the world."
>
> Psalm 46:10 (NLT)

JOURNAL APPLICATION:

Take a career interest survey. Identify the areas that you
want to work in. Prepare a résumé that portrays your interest
survey. Write down your commitment to submit résumés
and send follow-up letters weekly. Ex: I commit to sending
out five resumes weekly until I am successfully employed.

_____

_____

_____

_____

_____

_____

_____

_____

_____

_____

_____

_____

_____

_____

SECTION 6: FINANCES

"Lord, you have instructed me to bless someone financially. My spirit says yes but my flesh says no! Help! I don't want my blessings to pass me by because I was not obedient."

Obedience beats sacrifice. Walking in the will of God will always beat learning the hard way. Sometimes instead of pondering back and forth you should just do it! Be careful to entertain strangers; they might be angels.

"Dear Lord, I am thankful that I can hear your still voice and can be moved to act in obedience. Thank you for blessing me so much that I can bless someone else. I now understand that only what I do for you will last. Amen."

> Don't forget to show hospitality to strangers, for some who have done this have entertained angels without realizing it!
>
> Hebrews 13:2 (NLT)

JOURNAL APPLICATION:

When you want to bless someone financially write their name down and ask God to show you how to bless them.

_____

_____

_____

_____

_____

_____

_____

_____

_____

_____

_____

_____

_____

_____

_____

_____

_____

SECTION 7: SINGLE-PARENTING

"I am a single parent trying to make ends meet, Lord. Today things are not adding up financially and I am overwhelmed! What bills should I pay? Food and shelter are necessities. Help!"

*L*et your requests be known to God. Tell God exactly what your needs and desires are. Don't panic, God's got your back. Stay calm so that you can remain focused on the priorities of your household.

"Dear Lord, I pray for the anxiety and overwhelmed feelings to leave. I ask for wisdom and guidance to make sound financial decisions and to guide me toward resources that can benefit my situation. Lord, I may be single but I know that with you I am never totally single. Thanks for the provisions you are making for me and my household. Amen."

> Don't worry about anything; instead, pray about everything. Tell God what you need, and thank him for all he has done.
>
> Philippians 4:6 (NLT)

JOURNAL APPLICATION:

Write down the needs of your household in one column. Now write down the desires in the other column. Then write a prayer asking God to meet the needs of both.

_____

_____

_____

_____

_____

_____

_____

_____

_____

_____

_____

_____

_____

_____

_____

_____

SECTION 8: FORGIVENESS

"I have been unkind to someone who has treated me badly. I know that I am called to do what you would do, Jesus. However, this person pushed me over the edge and I am angry. Help, I feel terrible. Dear Lord, forgive me for what I have done and create in me a clean heart. Amen."

*J*esus is a restorer. He does not hold on to past hurts. Let yourself off the hook. Even though you felt like this person pushed you over the edge that does not give you the right to behave negatively.

"Dear Lord, please forgive me for my poor behavior. I acknowledge my hurtful behavior and pray that not only for you to forgive me, but for the person I offended to forgive me as well. Amen."

> Understand this, my dear brothers and sisters: You must all be quick to listen, slow to speak, and slow to get angry. Human anger does not produce the righteousness God desires.

> James 1:19-20 (NLT)

JOURNAL APPLICATION:

Write down the person's name you offended and write an apology prayer to them.

_____

_____

_____

_____

_____

_____

_____

_____

_____

_____

_____

_____

_____

_____

_____

_____

_____

_____

SECTION 8: FORGIVENESS

"I need to forgive someone who has violated me. Help."

Forgiveness is an area that many would rather keep quiet about. However, unforgiveness destroys families and can self-torment. Take a step toward forgiveness by forgiving yourself first.

"Dear Lord, my heart has been heavy for the burden of unforgivingness that it bears. I thank you in advance for taking this burden off of my heart and creating in me a clean heart. Lord you understand how badly I was hurt in this situation and how difficult it has been for me. You have forgiven me for wrongs. Now, please give me a spirit of forgiveness. I receive it and will walk in it. Amen."

> But when you are praying, first forgive anyone you are holding a grudge against, so that your Father in heaven will forgive your sins, too.
>
> Mark 11:25 (NLT)

JOURNAL APPLICATION:

Write out a plan to forgive those who hurt you. Write down their names and pray over them. Hold yourself accountable by writing the date and time you prayed for them.

_____

_____

_____

_____

_____

_____

_____

_____

_____

_____

_____

_____

_____

_____

_____

SECTION 8: FORGIVENESS

"I have acted unkind and evil; I know better, but how do I make this right?"

Confess your unkind deeds to God and pray for guidance and direction to make things right. God is bigger than your unkind deeds and He desires for you to walk in love. Love covers a multitude of sins.

"Dear Lord, thank you in advance for fixing what I messed up. Amen."

> Most important of all, continue to show deep love for each other, for love covers a multitude of sins.
>
> 1 Peter 4:8 (NLT)

JOURNAL APPLICATION:

Write down your unkind deeds and then write an apology
letter to the person you hurt.

_____

_____

_____

_____

_____

_____

_____

_____

_____

_____

_____

_____

_____

_____

_____

_____

_____

_____

SECTION 8: FORGIVENESS

"Lord, I have not talked to a family member because of some hurtful words. I know better and they have reached out to me. I don't want to go another day without forgiving this family member. Can you help me get to that point?"

We are not called to be the judge of right or wrong. That is left for God to decide. Going day to day with hatred in your heart will eat your spirit up and cause you to act out in a negative way. When you forgive, you tell God that you are trusting Him to take control of the situation and to let His will be done.

"Dear Lord, thank you for taking this pain of unforgivingness out of my heart and spirit. I feel better already. I never imagined life to be this peaceful until you lifted this burden off of me. I do not feel the pressure to have this person in my life, yet the forgiveness keeps on blessing me in other areas of my life. I am now no longer easily offended by things. Thank you for restoring my family! Amen."

> Create in me a clean heart, O God. Renew a loyal spirit within me. Do not banish me from your presence, and don't take your Holy Spirit from me. Restore to me the joy of your salvation, and make me willing to obey you.
>
> Psalm 51:10-12 (NLT)

JOURNAL APPLICATION:

Write down the names of anyone in your past that has hurt you. Now write down a prayer of forgiveness to them.

_____

_____

_____

_____

_____

_____

_____

_____

_____

_____

_____

_____

_____

_____

_____

_____

_____

SECTION 8: FORGIVENESS

"I have said something horrible and hurtful. My tongue has really gotten me in trouble. No one was supposed to hear what I said. I can't deny what I said. Although it was hurtful, I have to make this right. Dear Lord, how do I make this right?"

The tongue is like a two-edged sword; it is sharp. You have to tame your tongue. Pray that God can direct your path and guide you to ask forgiveness of the person you have offended. Thank goodness for pencils in life and an opportunity to erase a mistake and start over. God gives us mercy and grace enough for each day.

"Dear God, I pray that you take the mistake I made and forgive me for allowing my mouth to get me in trouble. I am truly sorry and I now pray that you give me the words and courage to apologize for my actions. Amen."

> The faithful love of the Lord never ends! His mercies never cease. Great is his faithfulness; his mercies begin afresh each morning.
>
> Lamentations 3:22-23 (NLT)

Gina Washington

JOURNAL APPLICATION:

Write down your actions. The first step to healing is
admitting your actions and owning them. Now write a
prayer of forgiveness for the person that you offended.

_____

_____

_____

_____

_____

_____

_____

_____

_____

_____

_____

_____

_____

_____

_____

_____

SECTION 9: GRIEF

"I lost a loved one and the grief is overwhelming. I saw my loved one daily, I talked to them, and now I miss them, and I want them back with me. Help me to move away from a spirit of grief and loss so that I can move forward with my life. Ever since I have lost a loved one, my life has been at a standstill."

Grief is a normal feeling after someone has died. How you process that grief will depend on how you will heal. Trust that God intends for you to move on with your life and that He never makes a mistake. Stop beating yourself up with all of the "why's" and decide from this day forward you can no longer live a healthy life in this constant state of grief.

"Dear Lord, I declare that from this day forward I will no longer live in a constant state of grief. Just because I have decided to move on doesn't mean I don't love my special person anymore. Lord, I want normalcy back in my life. I realize that this means one step at a time and I am willing to take those steps. I will get out of bed every day and declare abundant life before my feet hit the ground. I love you Lord for healing me from this stage in my life. Amen."

For his anger lasts only a moment, but his favor lasts a lifetime! Weeping may last through the night, but joy comes with the morning.

Psalm 30:5 (NLT)

To all who mourn in Israel, he will give a crown of beauty for ashes, a joyous blessing instead of mourning, festive praise instead of despair. In their righteousness, they will be like great oaks that the Lord has planted for his own glory.

Isaiah 61:3 (NLT)

JOURNAL APPLICATION:

Write a letter to your loved one explaining how much you value them and tell them you plan to live a life with joy and not depression, grief, and sadness.

_____

_____

_____

_____

_____

_____

_____

_____

_____

_____

_____

_____

_____

_____

_____

_____

SECTION 9: GRIEF

"Dear Lord, I have lost a child. Life is not supposed to happen this way; I am supposed to die before my child does. Help me! I am overwhelmed with unbelief and grief. I really don't feel like being bothered with people at all. How do I move on without pushing more people away from me?"

God is ready to move you out of a constant state of grief. He does require you to do one thing; surrender all of your feelings to Him. Stop holding all of your thoughts and emotions in, assuming no one understands. God understands and is ready to move you forward. Just because you move on with life doesn't mean you will forget your child. God is ready to lift up the name of your child as a way for other families to move forward.

"Dear God, I surrender all! I know there is more for me in life if I could just move forward. Please guide my footsteps in the right direction to move out of this state of despair. I am ready and truly surrender this to you! Amen."

> Trust in the Lord with all your heart; do not depend on your own understanding. Seek his will in all you do, and he will show you which path to take.
>
> Proverbs 3:5-6 (NLT)

JOURNAL APPLICATION:

Write down three ways that you can honor your child in joy and pray that God gives you the strength to carry it out. Ex: donate items to the local thrift store in memory of your child.

_____

_____

_____

_____

_____

_____

_____

_____

_____

_____

_____

_____

_____

APPENDIX

ADDICTION RESOURCES
www.addictionresourceguide.com

ALCOHOLIC ANONYMOUS
http://www.aa.org

CANCER RESOURCES
www.cancercenter.com/

GRIEF
www.helpguide.org/mental/grief_loss.htm